Buon Natale, Salvatore

ALFRED R. CRUDALE

Illustrated by Sue Greco

This book is dedicated to the memory of my great-grandparents Salvatore and Rosina Saccoccio.

Buon Natale, Salvatore
Copyright © 2024 Alfred R. Crudale

Produced and printed by Stillwater River Publications. All rights reserved. Written and produced in the United States of America. This book may not be reproduced or sold in any form without the expressed, written permission of the author(s) and publisher.

Visit our website at www.StillwaterPress.com for more information.

First Stillwater River Publications Edition

ISBN: 978-1-963296-80-8

Library of Congress Control Number: 2024915431

1 2 3 4 5 6 7 8 9 10
Written by Alfred R. Crudale.
Illustrated by Sue Greco.
Published by Stillwater River Publications, West Warwick, RI, USA.

The views and opinions expressed in this book are solely those of the author(s) and do not necessarily reflect the views and opinions of the publisher.

GLOSSARY

Buongiorno (Bwohn-jor-noh) – Good morning

Buon Natale (Bwohn Nah-tah-leh) – Merry Christmas

Natale (Nah-tah-leh) – Christmas

Nonna – grandmother

Nonno – grandfather

Presepio (preh-seh-pee-oh) – nativity scene

Signora (seen-your-ah) – Madam, lady

Vigilia (vee-gee-lee-ah) – Christmas Eve

Zampognari (zahm-pon-ah-ree) – bagpipers

One very cold December morning, Mamma told Rosina and me to get dressed to go to the store with her. December in New York is much colder than in Itri, our small village in southern Italy. I helped my little sister put on her red coat, white hat, and her blue mittens. Then I put on my green coat, white hat, and my red mittens.

We walked from our apartment on Mott Street to Mrs. DeLuca's store on the corner of Mulberry and Grand Streets. Her store was small and narrow but it was filled with many things. Red, white, and green Italian flags, silver and black espresso coffee pots, large pasta bowls painted with pink and green flowers, and small tin cookie cutters in the shape of Italy filled her small, narrow store.

Hand Carved Nativity Figurines

Mamma greeted Mrs. DeLuca with, "*Buongiorno, Signora*," as we walked to the back corner of the store. There we found a large table filled with small wooden statues. Mamma explained to Rosina and me that it was time to prepare for our first Christmas in America.

We chose several small statues to create a nativity scene, which we call a *presepio*, in our apartment. We bought Mary, Joseph, Baby Jesus, two shepherds, four sheep, a donkey, and an ox. Mamma also bought a doll that looked like *La Befana*.

La Befana is a tradition we have in Italy. She is a very good elderly lady who, flying on her broom, brings gifts to girls and boys throughout Italy on January 6, which is the feast of the Epiphany, or the twelfth day of Christmas.

Back at the apartment, we waited for Papà to come home from work. After he arrived, we ate dinner and then showed him the small statues from Mrs. DeLuca's store. Papà gave a big smile and said, "Let's set up the *presepio*!" From a closet in his bedroom Papà took a large papier-mâché cave, which he had made while Mamma, my sister, and I were still living in Italy.

The cave was painted gray with patches of green and brown. Inside the cave Mamma placed a handful of yellow straw. On the straw Rosina and I placed Mary, Joseph, the donkey, and the ox. Mamma and Papà explained that we would not place Baby Jesus in the nativity until after midnight mass on Christmas morning. We then placed the shepherds and the sheep just outside the entrance to the cave.

To add to our excitement, Mamma and Papà gave us some happy news. "Nonna and Nonno will come from Rhode Island to spend Christmas with us," exclaimed Mamma. Rosina and I were so happy we began to jump up and down. This was going to be the best *Natale* ever.

As the weeks went by Mamma continued to add colorful decorations to our apartment. One week before Christmas, Mamma went to Mr. Rossi's fish market to buy dry salted cod fish, which she would prepare for our Christmas Eve *Vigilia* Feast of the Seven Fishes.

On December 22, three days before Christmas, Rosina and I woke up to find snow falling outside our window. We had never seen snow before, because in Itri it is too warm for snow. We were amazed as we watched the white fluffy snow pile up on the long streets below.

As the snow continued to fall all day long, Mamma and Papà looked very worried. The next day Papà told us that there was too much snow, so Nonna and Nonno would not be able to come to celebrate Christmas with us. Rosina and I were very sad.

To try to cheer us up, Mamma said, "Well if they can't join us for *Natale*, then they will certainly come for the feast of *La Befana*. I have an idea," said Mamma. "Let's prepare the dough to make struffoli. The mention of this delicious Christmas dessert brightened our mood.

On Christmas Eve night, Mamma, Papà, Rosina, and I sat down to eat our Feast of the Seven Fishes, saddened that Nonna and Nonno were not with us. We ate fried smelts, calamari, snail salad, roasted eel, anchovy fritters, spaghetti with clam sauce, and of course baccala, the salted cod Mamma bought from Mr. Rossi.

After dinner, we all walked to our church on Baxter Street to attend midnight mass. Standing outside, on the steps of the church, were two men playing the bagpipes. In Italy these men are known as the *zampognari*, or bagpipers. They represent the shepherds of the first Christmas. No Italian Christmas celebration would be complete without them.

Once we returned home, Papà announced that it was time to place the Baby Jesus in the *presepio*. He handed the small statue to me, and Mamma said, "As you place the baby in the manger say a little prayer and maybe you'll get a surprise."

As soon as I had placed the baby in the cave I heard two familiar voices say, "Buon Natale, Salvatore!" When I turned I saw Nonna and Nonno stretching out their arms to hug us.

"You're here?" I yelled.

"We arrived while you were still at mass," explained Nonna.

We all hugged and kissed each other, and then we sang "*Tu scendi dalle stelle*," the most popular Christmas song in Italy.

Our first Christmas in America was truly a *buon* Natale!

Struffoli Recipe

Ingredients for the dough:
2 cups of flour
2 tablespoons sugar
¼ teaspoon baking powder
Pinch of salt
Zest of 1 lemon
½ stick of softened butter, cut into small cubes
3 eggs, beaten
1 teaspoon of vanilla
3 cups vegetable oil for frying

Combine the flour, sugar, baking powder, salt and zest in a food processor or mixer. Add the butter, mixing well. Add the eggs and flavoring, mixing until dry and wet ingredients are combined. Be sure all ingredients from the bottom of the bowl are combined in the dough.

Form the dough into a ball. Cover with plastic wrap or a dish towel and place in the refrigerator for 30-60 minutes to rest.

Heat the oil in a deep pan to 350-375 degrees Fahrenheit.

Pinch off small pieces of dough and roll into ¼" balls.

When the oil is heated, drop the struffoli balls into the hot oil. Cook until golden brown, 3-4 minutes. Drain on a paper towel to cool. Be careful the oil does not get too hot! Continue until all the struffoli balls are cooked.

Choose a decorative plate to serve the struffoli.

Ingredients for the honey coating:
1 cup of honey
½ cup of sugar
2 tablespoons water or lemon juice
Decorative sprinkles

Heat all the ingredients for the honey coating in a frying pan, stirring constantly until the sugar dissolves.

Once the sugar dissolves, add the cooled struffoli to the honey mixture, stirring gently to coat all the struffoli.

Struffoli are traditionally arranged in the shape of a wreath or mounded to represent a Christmas tree.

To make a wreath: Place a drinking glass, lightly coated with vegetable oil, in the center of the plate. Place the honey coated struffoli around the glass to create a wreath shape. When all the struffoli are placed around the glass, remove the glass.

To make a Christmas tree shape: Create a circle shaped base on the plate and then keep adding the struffoli to make a mound of struffoli, to represent a Christmas tree.

For both the wreath and the tree—gently sprinkle with colorful candy sprinkles.

Let cool and enjoy!

Recipe provided by Barbara J. Crudale

Lyrics to
Tu Scendi dalle Stelle
(*You Come Down from the Stars*)

Tu scendi dalle stelle,	You come down from the stars
O Re del cielo,	O King of Heaven
E vieni in una grotta,	You come to us in a cave
Al freddo e al gelo.	In the cold and the ice
O Bambino, mio Divino,	O Little Child, My Divine One,
Io ti vedo qui a tremar.	I see you here trembling
O Dio beato,	O Blessed God,
Ma quanto ti costò	How much it has cost you
L'avermi amato.	To have loved me.

You can listen to *Tu Scendi dalle Stelle* at:
www.soundcloud.com/public-domain-official/
tu-scendi-dalle-stelle

ABOUT THE AUTHOR

Alfred R. Crudale grew up in the Knightsville neighborhood of Cranston, Rhode Island. He taught Italian and Spanish for thirty years in the Warwick School Department in Rhode Island. He presently teaches Italian at the University of Rhode Island and Bridgewater State University, Massachusetts. He and his wife Barbara live on their small farm in West Kingston, where they raise goats and chickens.

ABOUT THE ILLUSTRATOR

A Rhode Island independent art teacher, Sue Greco has been instructing watercolor since 2015. Her workshops have taken her throughout the northeastern United States. In 2017 Sue published her first book, *Kids Best Watercolor Lessons* followed by *More Watercolor Lessons*. It has been a pleasure working with Al on his second Salvatore book. Visit www.suegrecopaints.com for more information.

Printed in the USA
CPSIA information can be obtained
at www.ICGtesting.com
LVRC101207231124
797434LV00019B/196